Third Grade
Dictionary Skills

MW01178797

Table of Contents

Introduction

When a child asks you how to spell a word or what it means, what do you do? Do you give the child the answers? Or do you tell the child to look in a dictionary? If you are a parent, giving your child the answers may seem like the kind thing to do. Sometimes it is the easier thing to do. But learning the skills required to use a dictionary, even for young children and students, is essential to their becoming independent readers.

Students remember what they read better than what they are told. Finding a word in the dictionary will reinforce the word, its spelling, and its meaning in a student's mind. Simply writing the letters as someone else dictates them does not offer the same opportunity for reinforcement.

Dictionary skills are also useful across the curriculum and in real-life situations. Learning how to find words by sounding them out and using alphabetical order helps students to use indexes, glossaries, encyclopedias, phone books, and other reference books. Looking up meanings and choosing the correct meaning of an unknown word through context help a student to become an independent reader in all subjects.

Use

Third Grade Dictionary Skills is designed to supplement the language arts curriculum. However, many pages concentrate on other areas of the curriculum, such as science, art, health and PE, math, and social studies. There are icons on these pages to help the teacher integrate *Dictionary Skills* into these areas.

At the third-grade level, the skills required to use a dictionary are reviewed, and students are given the opportunity for practice. The units, Alphabetical Order, Parts of Speech, Multiple Meanings, and Using a Dictionary, are meant to ease young students into the practice of using a dictionary independently. A dictionary designed for young readers is recommended as a companion to this workbook.

Most pages introduce a topic with examples and then provide practice. Some pages include a section called "Take Another Step," which encourages students to apply what they have learned.

The Glossary on page 3 is meant to help the teacher and the students as they use this book. The Dictionary Page Diagram on page 4 can be enlarged, laminated, copied, or simply posted in an area for easy reference. The assessment on pages 5–6 can be used as a pretest or a posttest to gauge learning.

It is hoped that students will have fun while improving their dictionary skills. Fun titles and topics of interest are meant to engage young students in learning. Devote part of a bulletin board to dictionary skills and display students' work. Encourage discussions and the use of the dictionary whenever the opportunity presents itself. Most of all, have fun!

Glossary

alphabetical order in the order of the alphabet; ordered from A to Z.

adjective (adj.) a word that describes a noun.

adverb (adv.) a word that describes a verb or an adjective.

contraction (contr.) two words written as one, usually with an apostrophe in place of the missing letters.

definition the meaning of a word.

dictionary a book of words in alphabetical order that shows how to spell the words and tells their meanings.

entry word a word defined in a dictionary.

guide words words printed at the top of a page in a dictionary, usually the first and last entry words on that page.

homographs words with the same spellings but different meanings, and sometimes different pronunciations.

noun (n.) a word that names a person, place, or thing.

part of speech a group of words in a language to which a word can be added; a class of words.

prefix a group of letters added to the beginning of a root word to change its meaning.

pronoun (pron.) a word that takes the place of another noun or a group of nouns.

pronunciation key phonetic spellings to help readers to pronounce words.

root word a word to which a prefix or suffix can be added to change its meaning.

suffix a group of letters added to the end of a root word to change its meaning.

verb (v.) a word that shows action.

Dictionary Page Diagram

entry words words that are defined

guide words first and last entry words on a page

numbers to show different words with same spelling

example sentence helps explain meaning

pronunciation key helps reader to pronounce words

definition meaning of a word

letter or letters to show **part of speech**

numbers to show different meanings

pronunciation key explains symbols that show how to say words

page number number of page in dictionary

---

click/code

clog¹ **v.** to block. Please don't clog the drain.

clog² **n.** a heavy, wooden shoe.

close¹ (klōs) **adj.** 1. near. 2. having a strong bond with someone. I am close to my best friend. 3. with little difference between two things. It was a close race. 4. careful. Take a close look. 5. warm and stuffy.

close² (klōz) **v.** 1. to shut. 2. to end. The day came to a close.

cloud n. (kloud) a mass of water droplets in the sky; usually gray or white.

a	add	**i**	it	**o͝o** took	**oi** oil
ā	ace	**ī**	ice	**o͞o** pool	**ou** pout
â	care	**o**	odd	**u** up	**ng** ring
ä	palm	**ō**	open	**û** burn	**th** thin
e	end	**ô**	order	**yo͞o** fuse	**th** this
ē	equal				**zh** vision

ə = { a in *above*   e in *sicken*   i in *possible*
      o in *melon*   u in *circus*

HBJ School Dictionary

51

Show What You Know

Directions: Look at the sample dictionary page. Use the sample to answer the questions.

---

stamp/trust

stamp[1] [stamp] **n.** a mark or seal.

stamp[2] [stamp] **v.** to bring your foot down with force.

track[1] [trak] **n.** 1. marks left by a person, an animal, or a thing. 2. a beaten trail. 3. a pair of metal rails, as a train track.

track[2] [trak] **v.** to follow by using traces left behind. The dog will track the fox.

trust [trust] **v.** to believe that something or someone is honest. Can I trust you to behave while I am gone?

---

1. What are the guide words on this page? _____

2. How many entry words are on this page? _____

3. What part of speech is **stamp** when it means "a mark or seal"?

_____

4. Write one of the example sentences from the sample. _____

_____

5. Which word means "a beaten trail"? _____

6. Which word shows more than one meaning? _____

7. What is meaning 1 of **track**[1]? _____

8. What part of speech is **stamp**[2]? _____

☞ Go on to the next page.

Show What You Know, p. 2

Directions: Use a dictionary to answer these questions.

9. Find the word <u>stand</u> in the dictionary. What page is it on? _____

10. What are the guide words on the page? _____

_____

11. How many entry words are there for <u>stand</u>? _____

12. How many meanings are there for <u>stand</u> as a noun? _____

13. Write the pronunciation guide and symbols for <u>stand</u>. _____

_____

14. What is meaning 2 for <u>stand</u> as a noun? _____

_____

_____

15. What is the meaning for <u>stand</u> as a verb? _____

_____

_____

16. Write an example sentence for one meaning of <u>stand</u>. _____

_____

_____

Animal Order

a b c d e f g h i j k l m n o p q r s t u v w x y z

How do you put words in ABC order? Look at the first letter of each word. Which letter comes first in the alphabet?

cat   elephant
dog   ant

Since **a** comes before **c**, **d**, or **e**, **ant** is the first word in this group.

Which letter comes next? Write the words in alphabetical order.

ant   _____   _____   _____

Directions: Look at this list of words. Write them in alphabetical order. Use the alphabet at the top of the page. Cross out each word as you write it.

| panda | goat | bat | aardvark | deer | monkey |
| snake | tiger | frog | zebra | horse | cow |

1. _____   7. _____

2. _____   8. _____

3. _____   9. _____

4. _____   10. _____

5. _____   11. _____

6. _____   12. _____

Name _____ Date _____

Sport Order

How do you put words in alphabetical order when the beginning letters are the same?

Look at the words <u>skate</u> and <u>stick</u>. Which word would be first? The first letter, <u>s</u>, is the same. You have to look at the second letter. The second letter of s<u>k</u>ate is <u>k</u>. The second letter of s<u>t</u>ick is <u>t</u>. The letter <u>k</u> comes before the letter <u>t</u>, so the word <u>skate</u> comes before the word <u>stick</u>.

Directions: Look at these names of different sports. The first letters are the same. Circle the word that would come first in each pair.

1. hockey
   hiking

2. bowling
   baseball

3. skating
   swimming

4. tubing
   tennis

5. basketball
   boating

6. climbing
   canoeing

7. skiing
   sliding

8. football
   flying

 Take Another Step

Write five of your favorite games or sports. Then write <u>1</u>, <u>2</u>, <u>3</u>, <u>4</u>, and <u>5</u> by the words to show ABC order.

_____   _____

_____   _____

_____

Name _____ Date _____

If the Shoe Fits

What if the first two, three, or even four letters of a word are
the same? You must keep looking to find the letters that are different.

shoelace   **shoemaker**

Both of these words begin with **shoe**. The fifth letter in **shoelace** is **l**.
The fifth letter in **shoemaker** is **m**. Since **l** comes before **m** in ABC
order, **shoelace** comes before **shoemaker**.

Directions: Look at each group of words. Put them in the
correct alphabetical order. Write them on the lines.

1. squeeze _____

squawk _____

square _____

4. imagination _____

imaginary _____

imagine _____

2. fireworks _____

fireplace _____

firewood _____

5. computer _____

complaint _____

complete _____

3. football _____

footstep _____

footprint _____

6. distance _____

disturb _____

discuss _____

Name _____ Date _____

State Scramble

Directions: Here is an ABC challenge! Use your scissors to cut along the lines. Then, paste all of the states in ABC order on another piece of paper.

Here are some hints to help you.
Make piles of states that begin with the same letter.
Put each pile in ABC order before you begin to paste.
If the first word of two states is the same, look at the second word.

Texas	California	New Mexico	North Dakota
Georgia	Hawaii	Kansas	Missouri
Oregon	Maine	Wyoming	New York
Florida	Iowa	New Jersey	Nevada
Nebraska	Montana	Utah	Kentucky
Michigan	Alabama	Alaska	Massachusetts
Arizona	Colorado	Delaware	Connecticut
Louisiana	Arkansas	Idaho	Illinois
Indiana	Wisconsin	Vermont	New Hampshire
Ohio	Oklahoma	Washington	Rhode Island
Tennessee	West Virginia	Minnesota	South Carolina
Maryland	Mississippi	South Dakota	Pennsylvania
North Carolina	Virginia		

Day in the Desert

A **noun** is a word that names a person, place, or thing. A noun can tell about more than one person, place, or thing. Add **s** to most nouns to make them plural, or to make them mean "more than one."

Some **plants** have many **flowers**.

- Add **es** to nouns ending in **s**, **x**, **ch**, or **sh** to make them plural.
- To make most nouns that end in **y** plural, take away the **y** and add **ies**.
- When a noun ends in **us**, take away the **us**, and add **i** to make it plural.

scratch—scratches   fly—flies   cactus—cacti

Directions: Choose and circle the correct noun in each sentance.

1. In the desert, the (day, days) are very hot.

2. We walk along a sandy (trail, trails).

3. A (hedgehog, hedgehogs) scampers across the trail.

4. The (cactus, cacti) are very tall.

5. They have long, sharp (spine, spines).

6. The (branch, branches) of the cacti reach to the sky.

7. Small (bunch, bunches) of flowers cover the cacti.

8. Different types of (plant, plants) grow in the desert.

9. We do not see any (daisy, daisies) here.

10. We leave before the (sky, skies) gets dark.

Happy Hamsters

A **pronoun** is a word that takes the place of one or more nouns.

<u>Tina and James</u> have hamsters.
<u>They</u> have hamsters.

The pronouns <u>I</u>, <u>we</u>, <u>he</u>, <u>she</u>, <u>it</u>, and <u>they</u> are used in the naming part of a sentence.

<u>The hamster</u> ate some food.
<u>It</u> ate some food.

Directions: Read each sentence. Think of a pronoun to take the place of the underlined words. Write the pronoun on the line.

1. <u>Tina's hamster</u> lives in a cage. _____

2. <u>Tina</u> feeds her hamster every day. _____

3. Tina gives <u>her hamster</u> water, too. _____

4. <u>The hamster</u> needs a clean cage. _____

5. <u>Tina</u> has a brother named James. _____

6. <u>James</u> has a hamster, too. _____

7. <u>Tina and James</u> like to play with their hamsters. _____

8. <u>My friend and I</u> went to visit Tina and James. _____

9. <u>Tina and James</u> let us hold the hamsters. _____

10. <u>The hamsters</u> were very cute and soft. _____

Take a Trip

A **verb** is a word that shows action.

People **drive** across the country.
We **walk** to school.

Directions: ▶ Read each sentence. Choose a verb from the box to complete each sentence.

lands	lives	sleep	walk	hugs
eat	fly	take	smiles	ride

1. My aunt _____ very far away.

2. We have to _____ to her house.

3. We _____ a plane.

4. The plane _____ in a big city near my aunt's town.

5. We _____ in a taxi to her street.

6. My aunt _____ when she sees us.

7. She _____ everyone.

8. We _____ at a restaurant near her house.

9. We can _____ to it.

10. We _____ well after a busy day!

Take Another Step

Write five verbs that tell what you do each day.

_____   _____   _____

_____   _____

Name _____ Date _____

At the Zoo

An **adjective** is a word that describes other words.

An adjective can tell about feelings.
   That seal looks **happy**.

An adjective can tell how many.
   There are **many** animals in the zoo.

Directions: Read each sentence. Circle all of the adjectives. They will tell about feelings, colors, numbers, or size. Then, draw a picture that shows some of the animals described in the sentences.

1. The zoo is home to many interesting animals.

2. We spent two long hours there on a sunny day.

3. We saw three huge elephants spraying cool water.

4. We saw four wild tigers pacing back and forth.

5. There were five noisy, green parrots.

6. Six striped zebras ate green grass.

7. We fed seven tall, spotted giraffes.

8. Eight slow turtles sat near a shallow pond.

9. Nine silly monkeys were playing in the trees.

10. When it was time to leave, we were ten happy, tired people!

Take Another Step
Write five adjectives that describe you!

_____   _____   _____

_____   _____

Name _____ Date _____

Short Cuts

A **contraction** is a way to put two words together.

   is + not = isn't

An **apostrophe** (') takes the place of one or more letters.

are + not = aren't	was + not = wasn't
have + not = haven't	were + not = weren't
has + not = hasn't	had + not = hadn't
can + not = can't	did + not = didn't
do + not = don't	is + not = isn't

Directions: Read each sentence. Choose a contraction to use in place of the underlined words. Write the contraction on the line.

1. Liza <u>does not</u> want to eat her vegetables. _____

2. She <u>is not</u> fond of broccoli or carrots. _____

3. Liza <u>has not</u> been eating healthy foods. _____

4. Liza's body <u>has not</u> gotten stronger. _____

5. Liza <u>can not</u> be healthy without a healthy diet. _____

6. Liza <u>was not</u> always this way. _____

7. Liza's mom and dad <u>are not</u> happy. _____

8. Liza's mom and dad <u>do not</u> like what they see. _____

9. Then one day, they see that Liza <u>is not</u> eating junk food.

   _____

10. She <u>does not</u> mind eating healthy foods! _____

Adding On

Some words can be broken into parts.
A **prefix** is added to the beginning of a word to change its meaning.

Sue is happy.   Sue is **un**happy.

A **suffix** is added to the end of a word to change its meaning.

Don is help**<u>ful</u>**.   Don is help**<u>less</u>**.

The part of the word that a prefix or suffix is added to is called a **root word**.

<u>help</u>ful   un**<u>happy</u>**

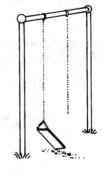

Directions: Read each sentence. Look at the word in dark print. Circle the prefix or suffix. Underline the root word. Write **<u>prefix</u>** or **<u>suffix</u>** after the sentence to tell what you circled.

1. Jill is **hopeful** that she will win. _____

2. The broken swing was **useless**. _____

3. Dee is **unable** to come. _____

4. That glass is **breakable**. _____

5. This baby bird is **helpless**. _____

Change the Meaning

Here are some common prefixes and suffixes and what they mean.

Prefix	Meaning
un-	not
re-	again
dis-	not

Suffix	Meaning
-ful	full of
-less	without
-able	able to be

Directions: Read each sentence. Underline the word with a prefix or a suffix. Tell what the word means. The first one is done for you.

1. The child is <u>unable</u> to reach the jar. __not able__

2. I will rewind the film. _____

3. My sister is unhappy. _____

4. Try to reheat your dinner. _____

5. Those flowers are beautiful. _____

6. The room was a hopeless mess. _____

7. I hope your shirt is washable. _____

8. Be careful with those dishes. _____

9. I dislike washing the windows. _____

10. That was a thoughtless thing to do. _____

 Take Another Step

Write two sentences about yourself. Use a prefix or a suffix in each one.

_____

_____

Name _____ Date _____

Now You Know

- -

- A **noun** names a person, place, or thing.   (cat, Joe)
- A **pronoun** takes the place of a noun.   (it, she)
- A **verb** shows action.   (run, drive)
- An **adjective** describes a noun.   (two, green)
- A **contraction** is two words joined together.   (it's, can't)
- A **prefix** or a **suffix** is added to a **root word**
  to change its meaning.   (helpful, helpless)

Directions: Read each sentence below. Then, read the part of speech at the end of the sentence. In the space, add a word that matches the part of speech. The first one is done for you.

1. Tony <u>ran</u> all the way home. **verb**

2. He _____ believe what he had found. **contraction**

3. He was keeping _____ safe in his pocket. **pronoun**

4. At home, he took out the _____ bone. **adjective**

5. He would add it to his _____ collection. **noun**

6. He was care _____ not to break it. **suffix**

7. Tony knew that fossils came from _____
   buried bones. **adjective**

8. The bones were from animals that _____
   many years ago. **verb**

9. Tony wanted to _____turn to the place where
   he had found the fossil. **prefix**

10. He looked forward to his next trip with
    _____ment. **root word**

Name _____ Date _____

What Does It Mean?

Directions: Some words have more than one meaning. Look at each pair of pictures. Read each sentence. Then, write the letter of the correct meaning on the line.

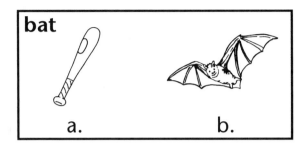

bat

a.   b.

pitcher

a.   b.

1. _____ Tony swung the bat at the ball.

2. _____ The bat is the only mammal that can fly.

3. _____ The pitcher stood on the mound.

4. _____ Please put water in the pitcher.

plant

a.   b.

light

a.   b.

5. _____ Jen showed us how to plant a tree.

6. _____ That plant needs to be watered.

7. _____ The puppy is quite light.

8. _____ The light will help us to see.

Art Smart

Directions: Read each sentence. Then, draw a picture to show what the word in dark print means.

1. Some birds **fly** a long distance each season.

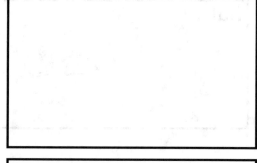

2. There is a **fly** in my soup!

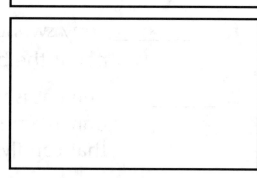

3. Please **set** your book on the pile.

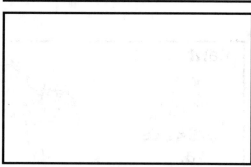

4. My mother bought a new **set** of golf clubs.

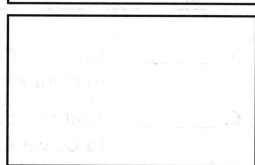

Pet or Pet?

In a dictionary, words with more than one meaning look like this example. Each part of speech has a number. If there is more than one meaning for a part of speech, each will have numbers, too.

pet¹   **n.** 1. animal kept as a friend. 2. a favorite.
pet²   **v.** to stroke.

Michelle has a **pet** turtle. (noun, meaning 1)
Teaching people to read is his **pet** project. (noun, meaning 2)
Meli loves to **pet** his puppy. (verb, meaning 1)

Directions: Read the meanings of each word. Then, choose the correct meaning for each word in dark print in the sentences. Write the number of the meaning you choose on the line.

cold¹   1. not warm.
cold²   2. a sickness of the nose and throat.
tie¹   1. to fasten together with string.
tie²   2. a cloth worn around the neck.

1. Please wear a **tie** to the show. _____

2. The **cold** water made us shiver. _____

3. Jane has a bad **cold**. _____

4. **Tie** a ribbon around the package. _____

5. It is **cold** and snowy outside. _____

6. David needs help to **tie** his skates. _____

Name _____ Date _____

The Trouble with Trunks

Some words have many meanings. Look at the different meanings for the word **trunk**.

trunk	1. the main stem of a tree. 2. the main part of your body, not including your head, arms, or legs. 3. a large box for storage. 4. the nose of an elephant. 5. storage space in a car.

Directions: For each sentence, choose the correct meaning. Write the number of the meaning you choose in the space. Underline the words in each sentence that gave you clues to the meaning.

1. Lori's **trunk** is longer than Sam's is, so she is taller. _____

2. Be sure to close the **trunk** before you drive away. _____

3. That elephant blew water from its **trunk**. _____

4. Let's try to reach around the **trunk** of this tree. _____

5. The car's spare tire is in the **trunk**. _____

6. I think my old toys are in a **trunk** in the attic. _____

7. The elephant uses its **trunk** to lift things. _____

8. The wind broke the **trunk** of that tree. _____

9. Your heart is in the **trunk** of your body. _____

10. Try to slide that **trunk** under the bed. _____

 Take Another Step

Draw a picture to show each meaning of **trunk**. Then, think of two meanings for the word **fall**. Draw a picture to show each meaning. Use another piece of paper or the back of this page.

Guide Words

- -

How do you find a word in a dictionary? First, you must remember to use ABC order. Then, you need to use **guide words**. Guide words are found at the top of each page in a dictionary. They tell you which words can be found on that page.

Here is an example: **spot/stamp**

The first word on this page will be <u>**spot**</u>. The last word on this page will be <u>**stamp**</u>. All of the other words on this page will come <u>between</u> **spot** and **stamp** in ABC order.

Would you find the word <u>**stack**</u> on this page? Yes. <u>**Stack**</u> comes <u>between</u> **spot** and **stamp** in ABC order.

Would you find the words <u>**swing**</u> or <u>**spill**</u> on this page? No. <u>**Swing**</u> comes <u>after</u> **stamp** in ABC order. <u>**Spill**</u> comes <u>before</u> **spot**.

Directions: Look at the guide words. Circle the words that would be on a page with the guide words. Draw a line through the words that would not be on the page.

1. long/move

lose	light
motion	love
marry	lost
needle	movie

2. safe/true

sunshine	sure
travel	taste
trust	sense
rule	trumpet

Name _____ Date _____

Guide Word Practice

Look at these guide words.

            crust/daylight

1. What is the first entry word on this dictionary page? _____

2. What is the last entry word on this dictionary page? _____

3. Which of these words could be found on this dictionary page?

Circle them.

crumb   crusty   damp   cry   dump   dare   cut

Directions: ▶ Write the word that would be on the same page as each set of guide words.

across   ill   dine   dad   job   arrow   ship   wonder

4. idea/in _____   **8.** cut/desk _____

5. apple/ax _____   **9.** serve/space _____

6. different/dry _____   **10.** able/ago _____

7. jar/just _____   **11.** wheat/wrong _____

 Take Another Step

Look in a dictionary. Choose a page. Write the guide words that are at the top of the page. Then, write three words from the page.

Guide Words: _____

Words on Page: _____

_____

Name _____ Date _____

Finding Words

Guide words help you find the right page of a dictionary. To find the word you are looking for, you must look at **entry words**.

Entry words are in **dark print** in the dictionary. Entry words are in ABC order. Look at this example page.

253
tiny/total
    ti•ny   very small.
    toad   a small animal that is like a frog.
    to•day   this day.
    top•ic   a subject in writing.

Directions: ▶ Use the example dictionary page. Answer these questions.

1. Which entry word comes second on the page? _____

2. Which entry word tells about an animal? _____

3. What does **today** mean? _____

4. What entry word means "very small"? _____

5. Could the entry word **tow** be on this page? Why or why not?

_____

_____

Name _____ Date _____

Many Meanings

- -

A dictionary may have sentences to show how to use each meaning. It also tells the part of speech, such as **noun**, that a word is. The part of speech is shown by a letter or a group of letters.

noun = **n.**   adverb = **adv.**

verb = **v.**   contraction = **contr.**

adjective = **adj.**   pronoun = **pron.**

bump¹	**v.** to hit against.
bump²	**n.** a part that sticks out.
burst	**v.** 1. to break apart suddenly. <u>The balloon burst</u>.
	2. to give way to a strong feeling. <u>We burst into laughter</u>.

Directions: Use the dictionary entries. Answer the questions.

1. What word can mean "to break apart"? _____

2. What part of speech is **burst**? _____

3. Which meaning of **bump** is used in this sentence, **bump¹**

   or **bump²**? _____

   Don't <u>bump</u> your head on the door.

4. Write a sentence for **bump**, using it as a noun.

   _____

 Take Another Step

Find the word <u>mine</u> in a dictionary. How many meanings do you find? What is the part of speech for each meaning? Write the parts of speech and the meanings here.

_____

Sounds the Same

Words that have the same spelling but different meanings are called **homographs**.

> **felt**—a soft kind of cloth
> **felt**—sensed something on the skin

Some homographs are pronounced differently.

> **wind**—moving air
> **wind**—to turn a knob on something, such as a clock

Directions: Write a new sentence using the homograph of the underlined word. You may use a dictionary if you need help.

1. Manny will <u>lead</u> Tony to the tide pool to show him the crabs.

_____

2. Manny has a small <u>wound</u> on his toe from a crab bite. _____

_____

3. Tony was pinched <u>last</u>. _____

_____

4. There is a <u>tear</u> in Tony's sock! _____

_____

5. Manny and Tony should not get too <u>close</u> to crabs. _____

_____

Take Another Step

Make a list of all of the homographs you can think of. Compare your list with your classmates' lists.

Name _____ Date _____

How Do You Say It?

One important part of most dictionaries is the **pronunciation key.** This helps you to know how to say new words. Each word has a guide next to it with symbols that show how the word sounds. The key explains what the symbols mean.

Look at this sample dictionary page and the pronunciation key below it.

event

event [i•vent´] *n.* A happening: The parade is a special *event*.

eventually [i•vent´choo•al•ē] *adv.* In the end: The snail will *eventually* reach the other side of the garden.

factory [fak´t r•ē] *n.* A building in which things are made.

fake [fāk] *v.* To pretend something is true or real when it really is not.

falter [fôl´ter] *v.* Hesitate: not succeed: He may *falter* when he tries to jump.

a	add	i	it	oŏ	took	oi	oil
ā	ace	ī	ice	ōō	pool	ou	pout
â	care	o	odd	u	up	ng	ring
ä	palm	ō	open	û	burn	th	thin
e	end	ô	order	yōō	fuse	th	this
ē	equal					zh	vision

ə = { a in *above*   e in *sicken*   i in *possible*
      o in *melon*   u in *circus* }

HBJ School Dictionary

Directions: Answer these questions using the dictionary page and pronunciation key.

1. How is the **tu** sound in **eventually** spelled in the key? _____

2. Look at the word **fake**. What word in the pronunciation key has the same vowel sound as **fake**? _____

3. The **e** in **event** sounds like the **i** in what word? _____

4. What word in the pronunciation key has the same vowel sound as the last syllable of **factory**? _____

Body Business

A dictionary
- has guide words to show which words are on a page.
- has entry words in ABC order.
- shows how to spell words.
- tells all of the meanings of a word.
- tells what parts of speech a word can be.
- sometimes gives examples of words in sentences.

Directions: Look at the example. Do what numbers 1–6 tell you to do.

---

blank/boss

blood   [blud] **n.** the red liquid that flows through the body.
body   [bäd ē] **n.** 1. the whole of a person or an animal. 2. the main part of a thing such as a car.
bone   [bōn] **n.** one of the hard, white parts that make up the body's skeleton.
bore   [bôr] **v.** to cause boredom.
            <u>Bill could bore anyone</u>.

---

1. Circle the guide words with red.

2. Underline the entry words in orange.

3. Circle the example sentence in green.

4. Put a blue **X** on the word that is a verb.

5. Draw a yellow line through meaning 1 of **body**.

6. Draw a purple line through the pronunciation guides.

The Meaning of Math

Directions: Use a dictionary to find the words in the chart. Fill in the chart with the information from the dictionary. Be sure to write the meaning that has to do with math.

Word	Guide Words	Part of Speech	Pronunciation Guide	Meaning
add				
count				
math				
number				
sign				
set				

Take Another Step

Write a sentence to show the math meaning of each of the words above. Use another piece of paper or the back of this page for writing.

Answer Key

Assessment

Pp. 5–6

1. stamp/trust
2. 5
3. noun
4. any sentence: e.g., The dog will track the fox.
5. track[1] (as a noun)
6. track[1] (as a noun)
7. marks left by a person, an animal, or a thing
8. verb

For questions 9–16, answers will vary according to dictionary used. Check students' answers.

P. 7

cat, dog, elephant
1. aardvark
2. bat
3. cow
4. deer
5. frog
6. goat
7. horse
8. monkey
9. panda
10. snake
11. tiger
12. zebra

P. 8

1. hiking
2. baseball
3. skating
4. tennis
5. basketball
6. canoeing
7. skiing
8. flying

P. 9

1. square, squawk, squeeze
2. fireplace, firewood, fireworks
3. football, footprint, footstep
4. imaginary, imagination, imagine
5. complaint, complete, computer
6. discuss, distance, disturb

P. 10

1. Alabama
2. Alaska
3. Arizona
4. Arkansas
5. California
6. Colorado
7. Connecticut
8. Delaware
9. Florida
10. Georgia
11. Hawaii
12. Idaho
13. Illinois
14. Indiana
15. Iowa
16. Kansas
17. Kentucky
18. Louisiana
19. Maine
20. Maryland
21. Massachusetts
22. Michigan
23. Minnesota
24. Mississippi
25. Missouri
26. Montana
27. Nebraska
28. Nevada
29. New Hampshire
30. New Jersey
31. New Mexico
32. New York
33. North Carolina
34. North Dakota
35. Ohio
36. Oklahoma
37. Oregon
38. Pennsylvania
39. Rhode Island
40. South Carolina
41. South Dakota
42. Tennessee
43. Texas
44. Utah
45. Vermont
46. Virginia
47. Washington
48. West Virginia
49. Wisconsin
50. Wyoming

P. 11

1. days
2. trail
3. hedgehog
4. cacti
5. spines
6. branches
7. bunches
8. plants
9. daisies
10. sky

P. 12

1. It
2. She
3. it
4. It
5. She
6. He
7. They
8. We
9. They
10. They

P. 13

Some words fit into more than one sentence, but best choices follow:
1. lives
2. fly
3. take
4. lands
5. ride
6. smiles
7. hugs
8. eat
9. walk
10. sleep

P. 14

1. many, interesting
2. two, long, sunny
3. three, huge, cool
4. four, wild
5. five, noisy, green
6. Six, striped, green
7. seven, tall, spotted
8. Eight, slow, shallow
9. Nine, silly
10. ten, happy, tired

Students' pictures should reflect the adjectives used in the exercise.

P. 15

1. doesn't
2. isn't
3. hasn't
4. hasn't
5. can't
6. wasn't
7. aren't
8. don't
9. isn't
10. doesn't

P. 16

1. circle <u>ful</u>;
   underline <u>hope</u>;
   suffix
2. circle <u>less</u>;
   underline <u>use</u>;
   suffix
3. circle <u>un</u>;
   underline <u>able</u>;
   prefix
4. circle <u>able</u>;
   underline <u>break</u>;
   suffix
5. circle <u>less</u>;
   underline <u>help</u>;
   suffix

P. 17

2. rewind; wind again
3. unhappy; not happy
4. reheat; heat again
5. beautiful; full of beauty
6. hopeless; without hope
7. washable; able to be washed
8. careful; full of care
9. dislike; not like
10. thoughtless; without thought

P. 18

Answers may vary.
Possible answers are:
2. couldn't
3. it
4. small
5. fossil
6. ful
7. old
8. died
9. re
10. excite

P. 19

1. a
2. b
3. b
4. a
5. a
6. b
7. b
8. a

P. 20

Check students' work.

P. 21

1. 2
2. 1
3. 2
4. 1
5. 1
6. 1

P. 22

1. 2
2. 5
3. 4
4. 1
5. 5
6. 3
7. 4
8. 1
9. 2
10. 3

P. 23

1. Circle lose, motion, marry, love, lost; draw a line through needle, light, movie
2. Circle sunshine, travel, sure, taste, sense; draw a line through trust, rule, trumpet

P. 24

1. crust
2. daylight
3. crusty, damp, cry, dare, cut
4. ill
5. arrow
6. dine
7. job
8. dad
9. ship
10. across
11. wonder

P. 25

1. toad
2. toad
3. this day
4. tiny
5. No. Tow comes after total in ABC order.

P. 26

1. burst
2. verb
3. bump1
4. Answers will vary.

P. 27

Answers will vary.
Possible answers:
1. That is a lead pipe.
2. The clock has been wound.
3. I knew that candy wouldn't last long.
4. Is that a tear in your eye?
5. Please close that door.

P. 28

1. ch$\overline{oo}$ or p$\overline{oo}$l
2. ace
3. it
4. equal

P. 29

1. Circle <u>blank/boss</u> in red.
2. Underline <u>blood</u>, <u>body</u>, <u>bone</u>, and <u>bore</u> in orange.
3. Circle "Bill could bore anyone." in green.
4. Put a blue X on <u>bore</u>.
5. Draw a yellow line through "the whole of a person or animal."
6. Draw a purple line through words in [   ].

P. 30

Answers will vary.
Check students' charts.